Lives and Times
Levi Strauss

Tiffany Peterson

Heinemann Library
Chicago, Illinois

Customer Service 888-454-2279
Visit our website at www.heinemannlibrary.com

Designed by Herman Adler Design
Map by Mapping Specialists
Printed and bound by South China Printing Company

07 06 05
10 9 8 7 6 5 4 3 2 1

Library of Congress Cataloging-in-Publication Data
Peterson, Tiffany.
  Levi Strauss / Tiffany Peterson.
      v. cm. -- (Lives and times)
Includes bibliographical references and index.
Contents: Everybody wears blue jeans -- The early years -- A new home and new name -- Dry goods business -- California gold rush -- Moving west -- Waist-high overalls -- Making better pants -- Growing business -- Family business -- Always thinking of others -- Growing success -- Learning more about Levi Strauss -- Timeline -- Fact file.
  ISBN 1-4034-3250-3 (hardcover, library binding) -- ISBN 1-4034-4256-8 (pbk.)
  1. Strauss, Levi, 1829-1902--Juvenile literature. 2. Businesspeople--United States--Biography--Juvenile literature. 3. Levi Strauss and Company--History--Juvenile literature. [1. Strauss, Levi, 1829-1902. 2. Businesspeople.] I. Title. II. Lives and times (Des Plaines, Ill.)
  HD9940.U62S777 2003
  338.7'687'092--dc21

2003002070

Acknowledgments
The author and publishers are grateful to the following for permission to reproduce copyright material: p. 4 Ariel Skelley/Corbis; pp. 5, 20 AP Wide World Photos; p. 6 Frank Boxler/AP Wide World Photos; pp. 7, 11 Bettmann/Corbis; p. 8 North Wind Picture Archive; pp. 9, 12, 15, 21 The Granger Collection, New York; p. 10 Jacqui Hurst/Corbis; p. 14 Hulton Archive/Getty Images; pp. 16, 17, 18 The Advertising Archive; p. 19 WarlingStudio/Heinemann Library; pp. 22, 25 Roger Ressmeyer/Corbis; p. 23 Thomas Houseworth Photo/Courtesy San Francisco History Center/neg. #8033; p. 24 Theophilus d'Estrella/The California School for the Deaf; p. 26 Gail Mooney/Corbis; p. 27 Morton Beebe/Corbis; p. 28 Robert Holmes/Corbis; p. 29 Levi Strauss & Company

Cover photographs by SuperStock, Brian Warling/Heinemann Library.

Photo research by Dawn Friedman.

Special thanks to Michelle Rimsa for her comments in the preparation of this book.

Some words are shown in bold, **like this.** You can find out what they mean by looking in the glossary.

Contents

Everybody Wears Blue Jeans

You probably have more than one pair of jeans. Many people wear blue jeans: adults, children, even babies. Jeans are popular with people all over the world.

All kinds of people wear jeans.

Jeans were first made for people who had tough jobs. They needed pants that would not rip or fall apart. The man who made them was Levi Strauss.

Levi Strauss started making jeans in 1873.

The Early Years

This house is where the Strauss family lived in Buttenheim.

Levi Strauss was born on February 26, 1829, in Buttenheim, Germany. His name was not Levi, though. It was Loeb. Loeb's father sold **dry goods.** He walked through town selling household items.

When Loeb was sixteen, his father died. Two years later, his mother, sisters, and he decided to move to the United States.

Loeb's older brothers, Jonas and Louis, had moved to New York earlier.

A New Home and New Name

The Strauss family took a ship to New York. The trip lasted more than a month. Because they were poor, they had to stay in a crowded room with no windows.

The Strauss family traveled to the United States in a ship like this one.

Levi explored New York. He loved his new country and quickly learned to speak English.

Loeb was an unusual name in the United States. When his family arrived in the United States, Loeb was given a more common name: Levi.

Dry Goods Business

Levi's brothers sold **dry goods** in New York, as their father had done in Germany. They taught Levi the business. Levi sold dry goods from a bag he carried on his back.

Levi sold dry goods such as needles and thread, spoons, and pots.

Levi knew he would have less **competition** outside of the city. It was hard work, but he learned that he enjoyed traveling. He went three states southwest to Kentucky selling his goods.

Many people sold dry goods in the city.

California Gold Rush

While in Kentucky, Levi began hearing stories about the California **gold rush.** Thousands of people were making the long journey to California. They wanted to find gold. They wanted to be rich.

Levi heard stories about the gold miners in California.

Levi went to visit his brothers who had opened their own store in New York. He did not stay long. He packed up supplies from his brothers' store and left on a ship for California.

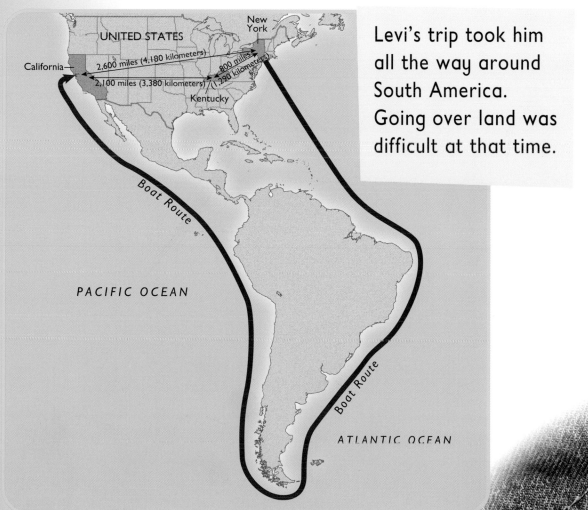

Levi's trip took him all the way around South America. Going over land was difficult at that time.

Moving West

Levi arrived in San Francisco in March 1853. His sister Fanny and her husband moved there, too. Together, they started a **dry goods** business with the supplies from New York.

San Francisco was a growing city when Levi arrived.

Many gold miners lived in tents until they found gold.

According to a Levi's Company legend, Levi brought a lot of **canvas** to California. He thought gold miners would need canvas to make tents.

Waist-High Overalls

Instead of tents, the miners said they needed strong pants. Levi had an idea. He asked a tailor to make pants from the thick **canvas** material he had.

Levi's first pants were made from tan canvas.

Levi's idea worked. The finished pants were strong. Miners liked them because they did not tear easily. Levi soon became famous all over California. His pants were called Levi Strauss **waist-high overalls.**

Miners called the Levi Strauss waist-high overalls "Levi's pants."

Making Better Pants

A tailor named Jacob Davis used **rivets** to make pants pockets stronger. His pants were so popular, he could not make them fast enough. In 1872, Levi decided to use Jacob's rivets on his **canvas** pants.

Levi and Jacob got a **patent** together so that only Levi Strauss & Company could make riveted pants.

Levi came up with a **logo** for his pants. It was a picture of two horses trying to pull apart a pair of pants. The picture was burned onto small pieces of leather and stitched onto pants.

Levi's logo shows the strength of Levi's pants.

Growing Business

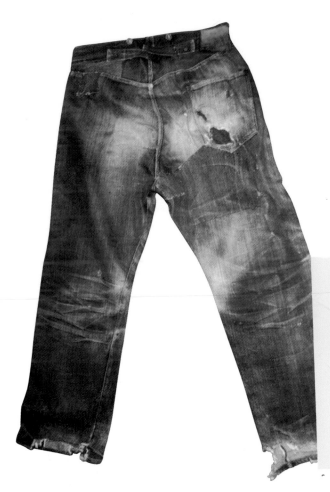

The Levi Strauss Museum in San Francisco has pairs of Levi's jeans that are over 100 years old!

Levi worked hard to make his pants better and better. Instead of tan **canvas,** he started making pants from blue **denim.** His business grew.

Levi was becoming a rich and important man. He hired more people. He opened bigger **factories.** Unlike many business owners, Levi spent time with his workers.

Levi Strauss & Company had its own building in San Francisco.

Later Days

Levi never got married or had any children. Levi hired his nephews to help run his company. He taught them everything about the business.

A **factory** makes many new pairs of Levi's jeans at one time.

This is the synagogue in San Francisco to which Levi belonged.

Levi decided he wanted to use his money to help people. Each year he gave money to his **synagogue.** The money paid for gold medals that were given to the best students.

The Company Goes On

In 1902, Levi Strauss became ill. He died on September 26. Even after death, Levi Strauss helped others. He left money to homes for children and for elderly people.

Levi gave money to schools including the California School for the Deaf, shown here.

When Levi died, his nephews made sure his company continued to grow. They began making things besides jeans. Levi's now makes pants, shirts, and baby clothes.

Levi's jeans continue to be popular.

The Company Today

Stores that sell only Levi's products, such as this one, can be found in 38 states.

Today, Levi Strauss & Company is still run by members of Levi's family. Levi's jeans and other clothes can be found all over the world.

Levi's jeans are sold in more than 160 countries. The company has more than 12,000 workers worldwide.

Levi Plaza in San Francisco is the main office of the company in the United States.

Helping People

Levi Strauss's name lives on. He is best known for making blue **denim** jeans. He is also remembered for helping others. Levi believed that school was very important.

In 1897, Levi started 28 yearly **scholarships** at the University of California, Berkeley.

In 1952, Levi Strauss & Company created the Levi Strauss Foundation. A foundation is a group that helps others. The Levi Strauss Foundation gives money to help children all over the world go to school.

The foundation also supports community art projects and education programs.

Fact File

- Levi Strauss's childhood home in Buttenheim is now a museum.

- Levi Strauss & Co. still owns one of Levi's first factories in San Francisco.

- The fabric Levi used to make pants was first called *serge de Nimes*. That meant the fabric was from Nimes, France. The name was later shortened to **denim.**

- "501" was the number given to the denim used for the first Levi's jeans.

- In 1906, an earthquake destroyed the Levi Strauss & Company offices and factories. New buildings were soon built.

Timeline

February 26, 1829   Loeb Strauss is born in Buttenheim, Germany

1847   Loeb, his mother, and his sisters move to the United States; Loeb's name becomes Levi

1848   Levi moves to Kentucky

1853   Levi moves to California

1854   Levi opens his first store in San Francisco

1866   Levi Strauss & Company moves into its first offices and **factory**

1873   Levi Strauss and Jacob Davis get a **patent** for **rivets** and begin adding them to Levi's pants

September 26, 1902   Levi dies at the age of 73

Glossary

canvas strong, thick fabric used to make tents

competition people selling the same product as someone else

denim strong, cotton fabric that is usually blue

dry goods household items such as cloth, thread, and needles

factory place where things are made

gold rush when a lot of people move to an area to try to find gold

logo picture that stands for a product

patent legal paper given to a person that says he or she is the only person allowed to make a certain invention unless he or she gives permission to someone else

rivets metal fastener

scholarship money given to a student to help pay for school

synagogue building used by Jewish people as a place for worship and for classes about religion

waist-high overalls original name for jeans; any loose-fitting pants

More Books to Read

Harper, Charise Mericle. *Imaginative Inventions.* Boston: Little Brown, 2001.

L'Hommedieu, Arthur John. *From Plant to Blue Jeans.* New York: Children's Press, 1997.

Roop, Peter and Connie. *California Gold Rush.* New York: Scholastic, 2002.

Index